Jake Kicks

Story by Annette Smith
Photography by Lindsay Edwards

Rigby®
A Harcourt Achieve Imprint

www.Rigby.com
1-800-531-5015

"Here comes the ball, Jake,"

said Dad.

Jake kicked the ball.

"Oh no!" said Jake.
"I cannot kick the ball
into the goal."

"Look at me," said Dad.

Dad ran.

He kicked the ball.

The ball went into the goal.

"I cannot kick a goal,"

said Jake.

"I am no good."

"You **are** good, Jake,"

said Dad.

"Come on.

Run up to the ball

and kick."

Jake ran up to the ball
and kicked.

The ball went
into the goal.

"Dad!" shouted Jake.

"I kicked a goal!"